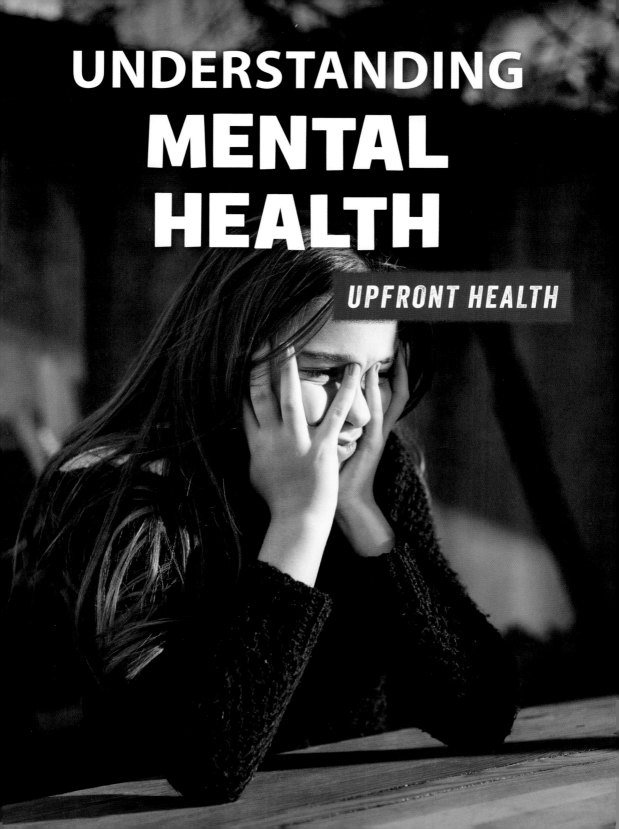

UNDERSTANDING
MENTAL HEALTH

UPFRONT HEALTH

Published in the United States of America by Cherry Lake Publishing
Ann Arbor, Michigan
www.cherrylakepublishing.com

Reading Adviser: Marla Conn MS, Ed., Literacy specialist, Read-Ability, Inc.

Photo Credits: ©EyeEm/Getty Images, cover; ©EyeEm/Getty Images, 1; ©iStockphoto/Getty Images, 5; ©Tero Vesalainen/Shutterstock, 9; ©Tetra images RF/Getty Images, 10; ©Kevin Winter/Getty Images, 12; ©iStockphoto/Getty Images, 15; ©Steve Debenport/Getty Images, 19; ©Maica/Getty Images, 20; ©Hill Street Studios/Getty Images, 23; ©Ssilverartist/Shutterstock, 25; ©iStockphoto/Getty Images, 27; ©EyeEm/Getty Images, 28; ©Hill Street Studios/Getty Images, 30

Library of Congress Cataloging-in-Publication Data has been filed and is available at catalog.loc.gov

Cherry Lake Publishing would like to acknowledge the work of The Partnership for 21st Century Learning.
Please visit www.p21.org for more information.

Printed in the United States of America
Corporate Graphics

ABOUT THE AUTHOR

Matt Chandler is the author of more than 35 non-fiction children's books. He lives in New York with his wife Amber and his children Zoey and Oliver. When he isn't busy researching or writing his next book, Matt travels the country bringing his school author visits and writing workshops to elementary and middle school students.

TABLE OF CONTENTS

CHAPTER 1

The World of Mental Health 4

CHAPTER 2

The Effects of Mental Illness 8

CHAPTER 3

Teens and Mental Health 14

CHAPTER 4

Solving Mental Health Issues 18

CHAPTER 5

Making Good Choices 24

THINK ABOUT IT.. 30
LEARN MORE 31
GLOSSARY 32
INDEX.. 32

The World of Mental Health

Seventeen-year-old Kevin Breel sat on the edge of his bed. Next to him was a bottle of pills and the suicide note he had just written. Although he was a popular student and star of the basketball team, Breel suffered from depression. To people around him, he seemed to have the perfect life. But all he saw was darkness, and he couldn't think of a reason to go on.

More than 16 million Americans suffer from **major depressive disorder**. It is the leading cause of disability for people between the ages of 15 and 44. It almost cost Kevin Breel his life. Fortunately, as he wrote his goodbye note, the

An estimated 300 million people around the world suffer from depression.

teen realized he had never talked to anyone about his problems. He never opened up about how he was feeling inside. How could he end his own life when he hadn't even tried to get help? Instead of ending his life, Breel changed his life forever that day.

Today, he has addressed his depression and become a national speaker. His TED Talk videos have been viewed more than 1.5 million times. Kevin Breel went from a teen on the verge of ending his life to a man who helps others believe in themselves.

Rural Living and Mental Health

*Did you know that the place you live can impact your mental health? People living in rural areas are more likely to be depressed than people in cities. Some experts say the isolation of rural living can trigger episodes of anxiety or depression. Also, for people who are struggling, help is hard to find. In 2018, 65 percent of non-**metropolitan** counties in the United States didn't have any practicing **psychiatrists**. Many mental health providers now offer telephone and video treatment options. This can benefit people who don't have access to a doctor or who cannot leave their home.*

Depression is the most common mental illness, but it is far from the only one. Anxiety disorders will impact more than 30 percent of adults in their lifetime. These can include general anxiety, social anxiety disorder, and **PTSD**, which is anxiety triggered by a painful event in your past.

Bipolar disorder is another common mental illness. People who have bipolar disorder have extreme mood swings. You might feel unstoppable one moment, unable to sleep, so excited and happy it is hard to focus. Then, without any reason or warning, you may feel incredibly depressed. It can feel like someone is sitting on your chest and you are overcome with sadness. These extreme highs and lows can be crippling.

For people experiencing one of these conditions, there is a lot of help available. Unfortunately, many people aren't getting the help they need. It is estimated that nearly half of the people who have a mental illness go untreated.

Depression in the United States

Out of all the countries in the world, the United States has the third-highest rate of depression among its citizens. More than 44 million Americans have some form of mental illness. And that doesn't include the people who are suffering but have not been diagnosed. What do you think is the cause for the high rate of depression in the United States? Do some research and find three factors that might contribute to the mental health **epidemic**. We know that where you live can be a factor, but what other reasons are there?

CHAPTER 2

The Effects of Mental Illness

Mental illness can have a major impact on the quality of a person's life. For a student, common mental illnesses like anxiety and depression can impact grades and lead to disciplinary issues in school. They can also keep you from playing sports and participating in other extra-curricular activities.

You wake up with tightness in your chest. You feel like your heart is racing, and you are drenched in sweat. You feel dizzy and nauseated. You are in the middle of a panic attack, but you have to be at school in 45 minutes. What do you do? Many people who suffer from a mental illness feel they can't leave the house. Interacting with teachers, classmates, and friends can

More than 2 million Americans experience
a panic attack in any given year.

become impossible. Multiple studies have found students
suffering from mental illness miss more days of school than
their peers.

Mental illness can be devastating to a person's social life as
well. If your friends invite you over after school and you say you
have the flu, everyone understands. But if you try to explain
that you had a panic attack earlier in the day and you are afraid
to leave your house, they likely won't understand. Many people
with mental illness report feeling isolated because of that lack
of understanding.

During a major depressive episode, a person may have problems with sleep almost every day for two weeks or longer. Some people cannot sleep well, while others sleep too much.

Then there is the impact on family. Families often struggle to understand and cope with family members who suffer from mental illness. Red flags in a child's behavior can often be overlooked by family members. People who are depressed may sleep a lot. They may become irritable for no apparent reason. They may lose interest in friends and social activities. People suffering from some mental illnesses may seem unmotivated and have rapid swings in their mood. When a child shows these signs, family members often describe it as, "just being a teenager" or some other similar answer. Sleeping a lot or being defiant can certainly be part of being a kid. But these issues can also point toward possible depression, anxiety, or other mental illness.

How to Help

Watching a loved one struggling with mental illness can be a helpless feeling. You may wonder, What can I do to help?

The biggest thing you can do is talk to them. People experiencing depression or anxiety often feel misunderstood. Ask specific questions and offer support. You should also do some research. Knowing more about their illness puts you in a better position to understand what they are experiencing.

Finally, encourage them to seek help. You might help them find a local support group. If a teen in your family is suffering, the National Youth Crisis Hotline (800-448-4663) might be a good option.

Dwayne Johnson battled depression as a young man. His mother has struggled with mental health issues too.

Success Through Mental Illness

What do U.S. Olympic gold medal swimmer Michael Phelps, singer Ariana Grande, and actor Dwayne "The Rock" Johnson have in common? Each has some form of mental illness. They have sought help, worked hard, and managed their illness to lead happy, successful lives. Many people attend therapy, take medications, and make other lifestyle changes to address mental illness. In virtually every organization in the world, there are people who experience a form of mental illness. They don't let their illness define them. They deal with it every day and work to live their happiest lives.

Children & Young People
Mental health problems often develop early

3/4
of all mental
health problems
are established
by the age of 24

1/2
of all mental
health problems
are established
by the age of 14

1/10
children
aged 5-16 have
a diagnosable
condition

Source: The five year forward view for mental health, Mental Health Taskforce, 2016

BBC

CHAPTER 3

Teens and Mental Health

If you are suffering from a mental health condition, it is important to know you are not alone. As many as 20 percent of teens experience depression, the most common form of mental illness. There is help available for you, and it begins with a mental health professional examining you and making a diagnosis. Unfortunately, studies show that as many as 70 percent of teens suffering with some form of mental illness receive no treatment.

Teens who have depression often perform poorly in school. That can lead to punishment in the form of poor grades, detentions, and suspensions. Imagine taking a young person who is already suffering and punishing them for something that is out of his or her control.

When struggling with mental illness, some teens self-harm as a way to cope with their stress, emotional pain, and out-of-control feelings.

When an adult is feeling sad, anxious, or depressed, they can make an appointment with a doctor to get help. As a child, you rely on adults to schedule your doctor visits. Since many teens are reluctant to talk to their parents about issues like depression, they may never get the help they need. This can result in children being confused. They may not understand why they feel the way they do. Experiencing anxiety or depression and not knowing what is happening can increase the anxiety a child is feeling. If a parent doesn't recognize the signs and take action, a child may suffer in silence.

When to Offer Help

Statistically, you know at least one person who has a mental illness. What if one of your close friends is showing signs? You may want to help, but there is still a social **stigma** *about mental health. You also don't want to offend your friend or make them mad. What should you do?*

If you think a friend may harm themselves, immediately tell an adult you trust. If you are worried about how they are feeling, don't be afraid to ask them. No one wants to suffer. Your friend may be scared to ask for help. You could be the support they need.

Would you feel comfortable talking with the adults in your life if you were feeling sad, depressed, angry, or anxious? Whether it is a parent, grandparent, teacher, or coach, you have adults who care about you. Don't be afraid to share your feelings. It can be the first important step to getting the help you need.

The rate of teens being diagnosed with depression and anxiety has risen steadily over the last decade. As strange as it sounds, that may be a good thing. Maybe more teens are asking for help. Hopefully more parents are spotting troubling signs in their child's life. More early diagnoses could mean more children than ever are receiving care to address their mental health needs.

How Social Media Impacts Mental Health

Social media is seen by many as a potential trigger for anxiety and depression. But one study found young people often turn to social media to ease their depression and anxiety. The chance to vent online is seen by some as a form of therapy. There are also plenty of real people out there waiting to help. Schools have counselors trained in mental health issues. Family doctors, therapists, and psychiatrists are just a few more professionals who can help. The key to getting help is finding someone you trust. A therapist can offer regular counseling sessions. A doctor may prescribe an anti-depressant or other medication.

CHAPTER 4

Solving Mental Health Issues

Once a person has sought treatment and been diagnosed with a mental illness, what's next? There is no one-size-fits-all approach to treating mental illness. What works for one person may not work for another. Ten people can be diagnosed with depression but show different **symptoms** and levels of the illness. Generally speaking, there are some common approaches to dealing with mental illness.

Hospitalization: If a person is suffering from **schizophrenia** or some other illness where they may be a danger to themselves or others, they may need to be hospitalized. Psychiatric hospitals are staffed with people specially trained to help. The person will also be given medication to help control their symptoms. Group therapy and

Medications do not cure mental illnesses, but they do relieve symptoms and help people live better lives.

counseling sessions are also usually part of any hospitalization.

Medication: There are medications that are very effective at treating depression, anxiety, and bipolar disorder. These drugs will be prescribed by a doctor who has diagnosed the condition. The most common drugs used to treat depression are in a class called selective serotonin reuptake inhibitors (SSRI). Serotonin is a chemical that transmits signals between the cells of the brain. People with a lack of serotonin show signs of depression or other mood issues. SSRI medications block the brain from reabsorbing serotonin, making more available to regulate

Seeing a therapist, counselor, or psychologist is common in the United States. Younger generations are more comfortable seeking out therapy.

mood. Most medicines have some side effects, so a doctor will do a complete exam and bloodwork before prescribing any medication.

Therapy: One of the best methods of treating depression and anxiety is to talk about how you are feeling. Family and friends can be great support systems. But therapists, psychologists, and psychiatrists are trained experts in mental illness. **Psychotherapy** gives a person the chance to share their feelings. You can talk about challenges you are facing at school, with your friends, or at home. The therapist will listen and reflect back to you thoughts on how you might improve the way you feel. Sometimes it takes an objective person to help you realize something and make an adjustment.

Studies have shown psychotherapy to be very effective. Have you ever been stressed out, but after talking to a friend, you felt better? Nothing changed in your life, but somehow talking about it helped you relax. Therapy can work the same way.

Mental Illness and Discrimination

*Students suffering from mental illness may face discrimination and harassment at school. The Americans with Disabilities Act (**ADA**) protects students from being discriminated against if they struggle with a diagnosed disability. But as we have already learned, half of the people suffering have never been formally diagnosed. This can make preventing discrimination more difficult. Let's say John is late to school three times in a month. His teachers don't know John is suffering from severe panic attacks and that is the cause of his lateness. If he has been diagnosed by a doctor, John may be legally protected from being punished. His anxiety is a disability under the ADA. But if, like half of people with depression, he has not been diagnosed, John's mental illness may lead to discipline at school. Can you think of other examples where you might face discrimination at school for a mental illness?*

The Positive Benefits of Food

One key to improving mental health may be found in the refrigerator! The science is called nutritional psychiatry. Doctors believe that what you eat can have an impact on your mental health.

Bipolar disorder is a brain disorder characterized by extreme mood swings. Doctors treating patients for bipolar disorder monitor what they eat. Caffeine, certain kinds of fats, and alcohol can all trigger bipolar episodes.

Multiple studies have also found a direct connection between healthy diets and significantly lower rates of depression. People who eat diets high in fruits, vegetables, and whole grains and low in processed foods have fewer mental health issues.

While many people know that nutrition and physical health are linked, some may not know that nutrition and mental health are also connected.

CHAPTER 5

Making Good Choices

The term "self-care" has become a popular buzzword. For many people, it means taking time out for yourself. Playing your favorite video game, taking a nap, or shopping at the mall with your friends may be ways you like to relax. You can't be your best for your family, friends, or at school if you don't take care of yourself. The same is true for your mental health. If you woke up one day and couldn't put weight on your foot to walk, you would tell your parents and go to a doctor. If you noticed a pain in your chest during gym class that wasn't going away, you would go to the school nurse and have it checked out. You need to approach mental health the same way.

Writing is a useful tool to slow down thought processes. Journaling can help someone think through a problem and find solutions.

Caring for your mental health begins with understanding yourself. Everyone has a certain amount of stress, worry, or anxiety in their lives. Only you know when the way you are feeling isn't normal for you. That is why self-monitoring is such an important part of good mental health. Self-monitoring can take many forms. Some people keep a simple journal. They track their feelings every day. This gives you a chance to record stressful activities or events in your life. You can note how you felt or responded in different situations.

Jobs In Mental Health

Does the idea of helping people feel better interest you? It takes caring, compassionate people to work in mental health. If you enjoy school, being a clinical psychiatrist might be for you. As a doctor, you would diagnose and treat patients with mental illnesses. Like psychiatrists, psychologists help diagnose and treat people. The difference is, they don't prescribe medication. People who suffer from mental illness have a higher rate of alcohol and drug use. As a substance abuse counselor, you could help people break their addictions. These are just a few of the fields where you would make a difference in people's lives.

A written journal allows you to look back and track patterns. Do you stress out more on Mondays? Do you have a panic attack every time you have to see a certain person? Patterns can help you identify potential problems.

There are plenty of apps for your smartphone that can help you self-monitor your mental health. Whichever method you use, recognizing problems before they get too big will allow you to reach out for help.

Almost 25 percent of military members report symptoms of at least one mental health condition. Having access to therapy options can help manage these symptoms.

Talking with trusted friends and loved ones and attending a support group has been shown to help people manage and recover from mental health issues.

Suffering from depression, anxiety, or any other mental illness is nothing to be ashamed of. Mental illness is no different than a physical illness. There are treatments to get better and ways to manage any disease. The most important thing is to never be afraid to ask for help. It is the first step to feeling better.

Genetics Play a Part

There are many factors that contribute to mental illness. Children who suffer physical or sexual abuse or neglect can develop PTSD, depression, and other disorders. Divorce, a death in the family, or the loss of a job can lead to depression or anxiety in adults.

Genetics *can also be a factor in mental illness. Children born to parents suffering from mental illness are more likely to develop a mental illness. There is no test that can tell you if your genes mean you will have bipolar disorder, schizophrenia, or depression. But these diseases often run in the family. Understanding your family history can be helpful in monitoring your own mental health.*

Think About It

Nutritional psychiatry is a new field of science. But people have long seen a link between nutrition and mental wellness. Many people have experienced the negative effect that certain foods can have on their energy and mood. These foods often include sugar and carbohydrates, such as bread.

Research this topic further using the internet or the library. How do different foods affect the brain? Do these foods affect young people differently than adults? Have you noticed a link between what you eat and how you feel, physically and mentally?

Learn More

BOOKS

Duhig, Holly. *Understanding Anxiety.* Buffalo: PowerKids Press, 2018.

Reeves, Diane Lindsey. *Health Sciences: Exploring Career Pathways.* Ann Arbor, MI: Cherry Lake Publishing, 2017.

Schwartz, Tina P. *Depression: The Ultimate Teen Guide.* Lanham, MD Rowman and Littlefield, 2014.

Spilsbury, Richard. *Bipolar Disorder.* Buffalo: Rosen Central, 2019.

ON THE WEB

HelpGuide Teenager's Guide to Depression
https://www.helpguide.org/articles/depression/teenagers-guide-to-depression.htm

KidsHealth
https://kidshealth.org/en/teens/your-mind/mental-health

MentalHealth.gov
https://www.mentalhealth.gov/talk/young-people

National Alliance on Mental Health
https://www.nami.org/find-support/teens-and-young-adults

GLOSSARY

ADA (EY-dee-ey) a federal law passed in 1990 protecting disabled workers from discrimination

epidemic (ep-i-DEM-ik) a health crisis that affects many people at once

genetics (jen-ET-iks) the process of passing down qualities and characteristics, such as physical appearance and risk for disease, from parents to children

major depressive disorder (MAY-jor di-PRE-siv dis-OR-dur) a mental illness that causes feelings of sadness and loss of interest in other people and activities; also called depression

metropolitan (meh-truh-PAH-lih-tun) having to do with a large city

psychiatrist (sye-KYE-uh-trist) a doctor who treats people with mental and emotional issues, usually by prescribing medication

psychotherapy (sye-koh-THAHR-uh-pee) a branch of medicine focused on treating people with mental and behavioral issues, usually by trying to change behavior

PTSD (pee-tee-ESS-dee) a form of anxiety and depression experienced after someone has seen or been part of a traumatic event; stands for post-traumatic stress disorder

schizophrenia (skit-suh-FREN-ee-uh) a major mental illness where a person may hallucinate or hear voices and live isolated from others

stigma (STIG-muh) a usually untrue or unfair belief that a group of people have about something

symptom (SIMP-tuhm) a sign or indication that a person has an illness

INDEX

Americans with Disabilities Act (ADA), 21
anxiety, 6, 8, 11, 15, 16, 17, 19, 20, 21, 25, 28, 29

bipolar disorder, 6, 19, 22, 29

genetics, 29

major depressive disorder, 4

panic attack, 8, 9, 26
psychiatrists, 6, 17, 20, 26
psychologists, 20, 26
PTSD, 6, 29

schizophrenia, 18, 29
self-care, 24
serotonin, 19
social media, 17
suicide, 4

treatment, 6, 14, 18, 28